KT-514-208

By Paul Mason

CONTENTS

INTRODUCTION

t *here are lots of reasons why you might want to improve your swimming skills. Some people swim as a way to keep fit, other people join swimming clubs. Maybe you want to learn to play water polo (football in the pool), to ride the waves on a surf board, or even train as a lifeguard! But the best reason for learning to swim well is that it makes it more fun.*

GUIDE TO TERMS

To help you understand the terms in this book
and the weblink, we have used the following...

'Arm stroke'   *the arm action that moves you through the water.*

'Leg kick'   *the action of your legs that moves you through the water.*

'Pull'   *the part of your arm stroke that propels you farther.*

'Overarm recovery'   *the part of the swimming stroke that takes place above water.*

Log on to www.activology.com
where you see this sign
to view live action clips.

SWIMMING VENUES

t here are lots of places you can go swimming, though you should always make sure that there's a lifeguard on duty. Most people swim in swimming pools. Sometimes these are set up for racing, with separate lanes, diving blocks and other equipment.

LANE LINES

These divide the pool into lanes. They float on the surface and help to make sure the racers swim in a straight line. In most pools these lane lines have special floats on them that stop waves going from one lane to another. These are called anti-turbulence lines.

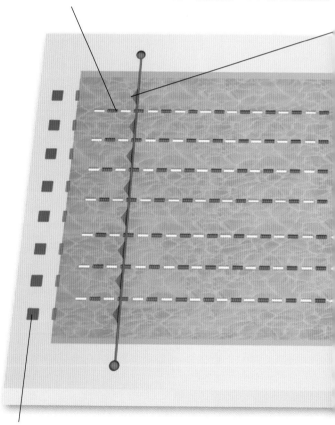

STARTING BLOCKS

These let the racers get a faster start. For front crawl, butterfly and breaststroke the swimmers dive off these starting blocks. In backstroke races they hang on to them while in the water.

FALSE START ROPE

This allows the starter to stop the swimmers if one of them has dived in too soon. If there is a false start the rope is dropped into the water and the swimmers swim into it. They know then that they have to go back and start again.

BACKSTROKE FLAGS

A backstroke flag tells backstroke swimmers when they are getting close to the wall. The swimmers count the number of strokes it takes them to get from the flag to the wall: then next time they go under the flag they don't need to look around to see how close the wall is.

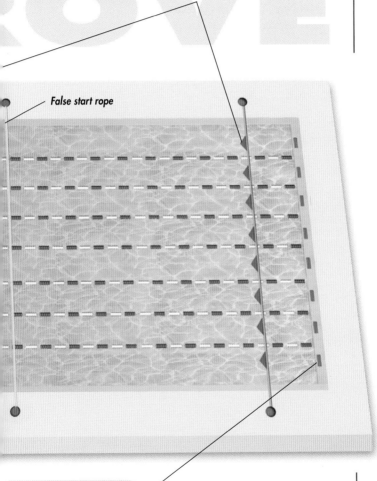

False start rope

TIMING PADS

When the starter fires the start gun, the clock begins to run. Each lane has a special pad at the end, which stops the clock when the swimmer's hand touches it at the finish of the race. The swimmer's time then appears on a large screen at the side of the pool.

EQUIPMENT

Swimming is a very simple sport which does not need much equipment. But there are several things you can buy to help you improve your swimming. Some of the best are floats you can use for practice using legs only or arms only. These help you to practise specific parts of your stroke.

SWIMMING COSTUME

Swimmers wear one-piece costumes. These are tight-fitting to allow them to move through the water more efficiently. Some swimmers wear special 'sharkskin' suits for racing. A raised texture on the surface of the material aids the flow of water along the body, making it more streamlined.

SWIMMING HAT

If you have long hair it's best to wrap it up in a swimming hat to prevent it from getting in your eyes. Hats also protect the hair from chlorine.

GOGGLES

These stop your eyes from getting sore and help you to see where you are going underwater. It's important that your goggles fit well: if you can, try different goggles before deciding which kind fits you best.

TOWEL

Always remember your towel! If you're going to be getting in and out of the water and drying yourself off between swims, it's best to take two towels. That way you have a dry one ready at the end of your swim.

KICK BOARD

These are used for swimming with legs only, which is a good way of practising your leg kick technique. Place it under your hands to support your upper body.

PULL BUOY

There are several types of pull buoy, but all are used for arm-only exercises. Simply place the buoy between your thighs.

GALA CHECKLIST

- Two towels.

- Tracksuit and T-shirt for keeping warm.

- Spare swimming costume and goggles for emergencies. (Take the spare goggles up to the start in case your favourite ones break as you put them on.)

- Swimming hat.

- Bag to put everything in.

WARMING UP

before you start a swimming session, it's a good idea to do some warming-up exercises. That way you will avoid straining your muscles and make an injury less likely. For swimmers, the warm-up should be in two parts: first, some exercises on the land, then do some gentle swimming before you start training in earnest.

LEG STRETCH

Stand back from the wall and place your hands flat against it. Keeping your right leg straight, bend your left leg at the knee. You should feel the muscles at the back of your right leg being stretched. Repeat with the left leg out straight.

PELICAN THIGH STRETCH

Stand with your feet flat on the floor. Lift your leg and hold it with both hands. Now gently pull your heel towards your buttocks. It's important to keep your hips level while you do this exercise: don't arch your back to try and get your foot up further! Repeat with the other leg.

SHOULDER STRETCH

Hold your right arm out straight in front of you. Pull it across the front of your body, using the inside of your left elbow to hold it in place. Repeat for your left arm.

TOP TIP

Whenever you are stretching your muscles, take care not to stretch them too much. You should stretch until you feel a very slight tightness, and no more.

SIDE STRETCH

Stand with your feet a little more than shoulder width apart. Keeping your body relaxed, lean to the left, trying to make an arc with your body and right arm. Lean as far as you can without straining. Repeat the exercise to the other side.

ARM STRETCH

Reach your left arm behind your head pointing down the line of your spine. Now reach your right arm up your back and up the line of your spine, and try to touch your hands together. Repeat with your right arm uppermost.

FULL-BODY STRETCH

Crouch down low with your heels flat on the floor and your arms out in front of you. Stand up, bringing your hands through in front of your body, until you are standing on tiptoe with your arms stretching up to the ceiling. Inhale as you go up, hold and then exhale as you return to a standing position. (If you can do this stretch underneath a roof that you can just reach standing on tiptoe, it will help you hold the position.)

FRONT CRAWL

f *ront crawl is the stroke most swimmers use if they are training for competitions or to get fit. It is the fastest of the four strokes, so you can swim farther in an hour doing front crawl than you would doing breaststroke. It is also known as freestyle.*

LEARNING TO BREATHE

This is a practice exercise to help you learn to breathe to the side. The basic technique of breathing while swimming is to inhale when your face is out of the water and exhale when it is below the surface. For front crawl you breathe to the side and for breaststroke and butterfly you breathe in front of you. Try to breathe on both sides if you can.

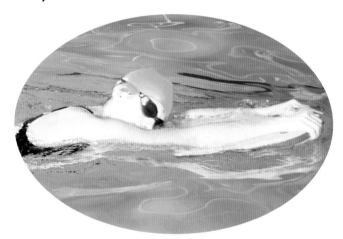

STEP 1   *Swim along using a float for support as you focus on the breathing technique. As soon as you need a breath, turn your head to the side. Take a breath and put your face back underwater.*

STEP 2
You can breathe out using the 'explosive' method (in one go) or gradually using the 'trickle' method.

FRONT CRAWL RHYTHM

The basic technique is to pull through the water with first one arm, then the other. Each arm comes back to the starting position as the other is making its pull. Your feet should always be kicking up and down.

STEP 1

After you have pushed off the wall, pull your left arm underneath your body, leaving the other straight out in front. As your left arm reaches the end of its underwater stroke, lift it out of the water. Kick both legs to propel you forward.

STEP 2

As the left arm starts to come through the air, your other arm pulls under your body. As your arm 'pulls' through the water, it propels your body forward and keeps you afloat.

STEP 3

The stroke is the same on the other side. Continue the leg kick, by kicking your feet up and down from your hips as well as your knees.

ARM MOVEMENT

In all strokes your hands should be cupped to 'catch' the water.

STEP 1

Extend one arm fully in front of you and feel the stretch as it enters the water. Note the tilt of your body as your right arm lifts out of the water.

STEP 2

As you pull back underwater, bend your arm at the elbow so that your hand is in line with the centre line of your body.

TOP TIP

Use an imaginary centre line, running from your head to the tips of your toes, to align your arms and legs correctly for the stroke.

FRONT CRAWL
CONTINUED

Once you have learnt the basic front crawl stroke, you can start to work on the arm movement. There are two main areas in which even good swimmers can sometimes make big improvements: the underwater stroke and the overarm recovery.

UNDERWATER STROKE

▷ The underwater stroke is where most of your speed comes from, so it's important for it to be as powerful and effective as possible.

STEP 1
Your right arm enters the water straight ahead of you. Before you start to pull your arm back, let your shoulder drop forwards slightly.

STEP 2
Pull your arm slightly away from your imaginary centre line.

STEP 3
Your hand can cross the centre line a little, underneath your body. The arm performs an 'S' shape movement.

STEP 4
Now pull back towards your hip. As your hand leaves the water, your other hand should just be entering it.

OVERARM RECOVERY

The overarm recovery helps keep your stroke smooth and your body balanced.

STEP 1
Lift your right arm out of the water with the elbow bent. Your left arm should just be starting its underwater stroke.

STEP 2
Continue to bring your hand forwards lifting your elbow slightly.

STEP 3
As your elbow reaches its highest point, your hand should be just reaching your shoulder.

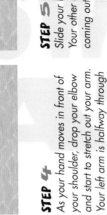

STEP 4
As your hand moves in front of your shoulder, drop your elbow and start to stretch out your arm. Your left arm is halfway through its underwater stroke.

STEP 5
Slide your hand into the water. Your other arm should just be coming out of the water.

Swim along looking at the bottom of the pool, slightly ahead of you. Your head should be positioned with the water coming just over your eyebrows.

TOP TIP

When you are doing your stroke underwater, don't rush. Instead try to 'feel' the water, catching it in your cupped hands. It is as if you are pulling a 'chunk' of water towards you and moving over it.

BACKSTROKE

*b*ackstroke is swum looking up at the roof or sky. Each arm pulls in turn, and people often confuse backstroke with 'upside-down' front crawl. One of the most important secrets of swimming backstroke well is to keep your head and body as still as possible.

BACKSTROKE RHYTHM

People learning backstroke sometimes dig their arms too deeply into the water. The underwater pull for backstroke goes to the side of the body, rather than underneath it. Your hands and arms only need to be deep enough underwater to be sure that your hands won't break the surface in the middle of your pull.

STEP 1

With your right arm at full stretch, your left arm should be just about to come out of the water.

STEP 2

Your right arm pulls through the water as your straight arm comes through the air.

STEP 3

Your hand is just below the surface during the middle of your stroke.

STEP 4

Just as your right arm gets to the end of its stroke, your left arm is about to enter the water.

ARM MOVEMENT

As your arms propel you through the water, keep your hips high and your body straight.

STEP 1

When your arm enters the water it goes in straight, with the little finger of your cupped hand pointing downwards (into the water). The palm faces away from you.

STEP 2

The arm that has finished its pull comes straight through the air. A strong leg kick will help you keep your body flat in the water.

HAND MOVEMENT

Your hand should go in leading with the little finger first. This is the best way, as your hand is already in the right position to start the stroke.

Your arms should be straight as they go through the air, and only bend after they have entered the water.

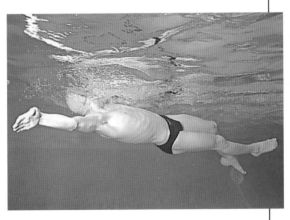

TOP TIP

Try to establish a breathing rhythm that is in unison with your stroke action.

BACKSTROKE

CONTINUED

a smooth, steady kick is very important for backstroke swimmers. If your kick is powerful it keeps your body in the right position in the water. If your kick is weak, your hips and legs will sink down. Your arms will end up having to drag the rest of you through the water like a weight, making your strokes inefficient.

UNDERWATER STROKE

Having a smooth, powerful underwater stroke helps you to keep your head straight in the water, which will help you swim faster. As in front crawl, try to keep the line that runs down the centre of your body straight. Twisting from side to side will slow you down.

The head is in line with the body

The arm pulls through the water at an angle.

STEP 1
Your right arm should enter the water fully extended.

STEP 2
As your left arm rises out of the water, your arm starts to sweep to the side.

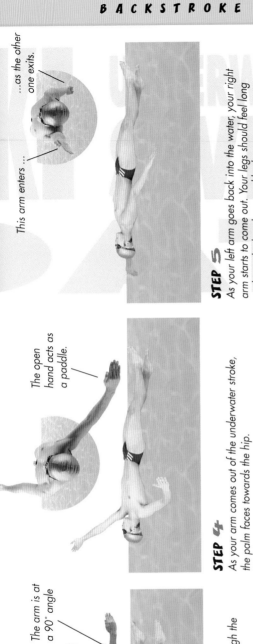

This arm enters ...

...as the other one exits.

The open hand acts as a paddle.

The arm is at a 90° angle

STEP 3
Move the right arm so that it is halfway through the stroke and at 90° to your body.

STEP 4
As your arm comes out of the underwater stroke, the palm faces towards the hip.

STEP 5
As your left arm goes back into the water, your right arm starts to come out. Your legs should feel long and stretched and your ankles loose.

TOP TIP

Keep looking straight up at the ceiling; if you find yourself looking back where you've just come from, you know that your body is in the wrong position in the water.

BREASTSTROKE

b reaststroke is often the first stroke that people can do when they start learning to swim. It feels comfortable because you can swim with your face out of the water. Breaststroke can also be an extremely fast stroke, if you can establish a rhythm of arm pull and leg kick.

BREASTSTROKE RHYTHM

One of the most important things to learn if you want to swim breaststroke well is when to put your face into the water. Swimming below the surface and the rise back up are what gives the stroke its rhythm and speed.

STEP 1
Start your arm stroke by moving them out and back in a circular motion. Your legs should be trailing behind you.

STEP 2
As you pull your arms in, your body rises up and your legs come back towards your bottom. Breathe in.

STEP 3
As your hands start to come forward again, your legs extend out behind you ready for the next kick.

STEP 4
Your body drops back down into the water.

STEP 5
Bring your legs forward and your feet to your bottom. Kick into the glide (see below left), ready to repeat the stroke.

BODY POSITION

As your hands come back in close to your body, your head lifts up and your legs start to get into position for the next kick.

TOP TIP

Always try to begin your kick with your heels close to or touching your bottom. Try to end your kick with your toes pointing back and your feet together.

GLIDING

After your kick, let yourself glide forwards with your arms and legs stretched out. Then, just before you start to slow down, begin your next arm stroke.

BREASTSTROKE CONTINUED

t here are two main ways of doing a breaststroke pull. Some swimmers let their arms glide forwards, keeping them almost straight until they power back in, to lift up the body. Other swimmers bend their arms almost immediately, and seem to be pulling back more. Neither way is better: just find the one that suits you best.

HAND MOVEMENT

Getting the speed right of your hands through the water is very important if you want to swim faster breaststroke. Some swimmers find that the best moment to sweep their hands in after the glide is at the moment when they can't see them in their goggles any more.

STEP 1

As you glide forwards, your hands are together before they tilt outwards, with the little finger highest.

STEP 2
Your hands sweep out, keeping up your speed from the glide.

STEP 3
Finally, your hands sweep in, as you bring your legs up ready for the next kick.

LEG MOVEMENT

Most of your speed in breaststroke comes from your legs. Although your arms drive you forwards, their main job is to get your body into position for the next leg kick.

STEP 1
After your kick, let yourself glide forwards with your arms and legs outstretched.

STEP 2
Then, just before you start to slow down, begin your next arm and leg strokes.

STEP 3
As your arms begin to move back, your legs move forward, with the knees leading.

STEP 4
Continue to bring your legs forward, while your arms complete the circular motion to return to the starting position. Keep your feet flat and facing out so that they act as a paddle to move you forward.

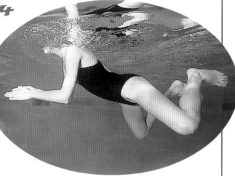

TOP TIP
It is important to get the timing of your kick and pull right. You should be gliding forward after your kick, then use your arm stroke to lift your body up ready for the next big kick.

BASIC BUTTERFLY

When you first start learning to swim butterfly, one of the most important things is to get your body position right. Try to stop your body sinking down in the water. If your hips start to sink you will find that your arms are having to drag the rest of you along. Your elbows will drag in the water during your overarm stroke and you will find it hard to take a breath.

BUTTERFLY RHYTHM

▲ The underwater stroke for butterfly is basically the same as for front crawl (see pages 12–13), except that your arms and legs do the same thing at the same time. The thing most people find tricky is the two-arm recovery.

STEP 1

At the end of your pull, your body comes up out of the water quite a long way. Your arms come out and start to swing forwards.

STEP 2

As your arms swing towards the front of your body, your head will start to drop down into the water.

STEP 3

Your face will just be going under. Your next pull needs to lift you up again.

DOLPHIN KICK

To do a butterfly kick, your feet and legs must be together. Your hips then move up and down and send a wave-like movement down your legs to your feet. The golden rule is to do one leg action as your arms enter the water and one as they come out of it.

ARM MOVEMENT

Getting the arm movement right is essential to time your breathing correctly.

STEP 1

After your arms have gone into the water together, about the width of your shoulders, they are ready for the pull.

STEP 2

As you pull back, bend your arms slightly so that your hands go under your body.

STEP 3

During the overarm recovery you can either lift your head to take a breath or keep your head down to do two strokes with one breath.

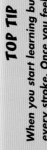

TOP TIP

When you start learning butterfly, breathe every stroke. Once you feel a little more confident, try to breathe every two or three strokes.

ADVANCED BUTTERFLY

Once you start swimming butterfly faster, your stroke needs to change from when you were learning. Beginners do butterfly as an 'up and down' stroke, with their head and shoulders coming a long way out of the water. The fastest butterfly swimmers concentrate on going along, instead of up and down.

TWO-ARM RECOVERY

One of the keys to swimming fast butterfly is how you breathe. Your head and shoulders should be in the same position the whole time, whether you are taking a breath or not. To breathe, you simply lift your chin forwards and take a breath, before dropping it back down.

STEP 1 As your arms come out of the water, push your chin forwards and take a breath. Your shoulders should stay quite low (compare this photo with the one on the previous page).

STEP 2 As your arms come forward your head starts to drop down. The shoulders are still low.

STEP 3 Your arms reach the front of your stroke as your head drops down again.

STEP 4 Your arms enter the water with the thumbs first and shoulder width apart. Breathe out.

UNDERWATER STROKE

The underwater stroke for advanced butterfly is similar to front crawl. Your hands drift out a little and make an S-shaped motion as they come in under your body and back out to finish the stroke.

STEP 1 Your arms drive forwards after the two-arm recovery, then swing out to shoulder width apart.

STEP 2 Your arms sweep out a little and then in towards the centre line to create this 'S'-shape movement.

STEP 3 As your arms power back, your chin begins to lift.

STEP 4 Lift your chin and take a breath as your arms emerge.

STEP 5 As your arms swing forward your chin starts to drop.

STEP 6 Your arms come forward and enter the water at the same time as your face.

LEARNING TO DIVE

Learning to dive is great fun, but always make sure you are learning in water that is deep enough and that there's a lifeguard on duty to help in case you get into trouble. When you start learning, don't worry about how far from the wall you can dive. The main thing is to try and get in the water making as little splash as possible.

STARTER DIVE

This dive is a good way to get the feeling of going smoothly into the water, instead of making a lot of splash.

STEP 1

Stand straight upright on the side with your arms up and your toes curled over the edge of the pool.

STEP 2

Lean forwards, lifting one of your legs up straight behind you. You should aim to be in a straight line from the tips of your fingers to your big toe of the raised leg.

STEP 3

Carry on toppling forwards into the water.

STEP 4

As your body goes into the water, start to bring your legs together.

STEP 5

Try to get your legs together and pointing to the ceiling before they disappear into the water.

INTERMEDIATE DIVE

Once you have got the feeling of going into the water smoothly, try this dive. Don't try to leap out as far as you possibly can: try to dive in with as little splash as possible.

STEP 1

Stand on the side with your arms out in front and your legs slightly bent.

STEP 2

Let yourself fall forwards, giving a little push off with your feet. Aim to hit a particular spot on the water's surface with your hands.

STEP 3

As your hands go into the water, start to lift your legs up and drop your hips slightly.

STEP 4

Try to make your whole body go through the same spot as your hands on the water's surface. It helps to imagine yourself jumping arms-first through a hoop.

RACING STARTS

In a swimming race, starts and turns are often what divides the fastest swimmers from the rest. A good start is important, because it is easier to swim your own race with clear water on either side of you. It also makes it less likely that your stroke will be disturbed by waves caused by other swimmers. Practise gauging the angle and distance of your dive.

STARTING SEQUENCE

In a race you use this starting sequence for front crawl, breaststroke and butterfly. With backstroke you begin in the water.

STEP 1 The referee blows short blasts on a whistle. This is your signal to stand behind your block. After the referee blows one long blast on the whistle you should get up on to your block.

STEP 2 Lean forward to begin the starting position. In a race it is important, at this point, to concentrate and stay focused on what you are about to do.

STEP 3 When the starter says 'Take your marks!', get into the starting position ready to dive in. The starter sets off a starting gun or a signal like a loud electronic beep. This is your signal to go!

THE PERFECT DIVE

Just diving out a long way from the block isn't necessarily a good dive. Try to make your dive as smooth as possible.

STEP 1

Dive forwards, but only to the farthest point you can comfortably manage.

STEP 2

Start to point your arms and head down towards the water. It might help at first to imagine yourself diving out and over something.

STEP 3

Your arms enter the water with your body straight.

STEP 4

As your hips go into the water, arch your back a little. The moment when you arch your back will determine how deep you go. If you arch it later, you will do a deeper dive.

STEP 5

Glide underwater, starting your stroke only when you feel yourself beginning to slow down.

WARNING

Always make sure the water you are diving into is deep enough so that you don't hit the bottom.

RACING TURNS

Perfecting your turns will increase your overall speed. The tumbling, twisting action of a turn requires power and speed from the momentum of your stroke.

FRONT CRAWL TURN (TUMBLE TURN)

The front crawl turn, otherwise known as the tumble turn, is much faster than touching the wall and pushing off again. Start your rotation approximately 1–1.5 metres (3–4 ft) before you reach the wall. It is important to time your stretch so that your arm meets the wall without gliding.

STEP 1

As you approach the wall (about one stroke away from it) drop your hands and shoulders down. Lead and the rest of your body will follow.

STEP 2

As your body tumbles round, your legs start to rise out of the water. Begin to twist on to your side.

STEP 3

Your feet hit the wall while you are still on your side. Continue to twist round as you start to push off the wall.

STEP 4

As you push away from the wall, finish twisting round so that you are on your front. Streamline your body by fully extending your arms and legs.

BREASTSTROKE PUSH OFF

In breaststroke, you can do one full stroke underwater before coming up for air. Once you have pushed off, pull through underwater. Aim to get a really big pull through, and then glide along with your arms down by your sides.

As you feel you are about to slow down, bring your hands back through underneath your body and get ready for your kick to the surface. Just as you reach the surface you can make your armstroke, and take a breath!

BREASTSTROKE AND BUTTERFLY TURN

The turn for these strokes is similar, except that the butterfly is done nearer the surface of the water. In both turns your hands must hit the wall level and at exactly the same moment.

STEP 1 Hit the wall with your hands together.

STEP 2 Pull one of your shoulders backwards – if you are right-handed, your right shoulder will probably be most comfortable, and vice versa. At the same time, your legs come in under your body.

STEP 3 Bring your other arm over so that both arms are out in front, ready for you to push off.

BUTTERFLY PUSH OFF

Position yourself on your front before pushing off from the wall to continue your stroke.

BACKSTROKE STARTS & TURNS

b ackstroke starts and turns are harder to learn because you can't always see where you're heading while swimming. Recently, the swimming laws changed to make backstroke turns easier and faster. The new-style turns are easier for non-racers as well.

BACKSTROKE START

The starting sequence for backstroke is slightly different from the other strokes, because you have to start in the water.

STEP 1

The referee blows short blasts on the whistle. This is your signal to jump into the water. These are followed by a long blast on the whistle. Swimmers must hold onto the block or railings with their feet flat against the wall.

STEP 2

The starter says, 'Take your marks!'. Pull yourself up ready to go. Your feet should be high but your toes should remain under the water.

STEP 3

Bang! You're off. Leap away from the wall and stretch out as far as you can, with your arms out above your head.

BACKSTROKE TURN

The backstroke turn is a slight variation on the front crawl turn. Use the backstroke flags (see page 5) to work out how far away from the wall you should turn. You will probably need to be four strokes from the wall.

STEP 1

As you get close to the wall, start to turn on to your front. Don't turn over too far from the wall, or you'll end up having to drift in towards it.

STEP 2

Once you are on your front you pull underwater as part of your turn.

STEP 3

As your arm goes underneath you propel your body forward to begin the turn.

STEP 4

Do a tumble turn; the first part of this turn is the same as for freestyle (see page 32), but you do not turn on to your front as your legs hit the wall.

STEP 5

Push off on your back and reach for the next length.

TOP TIP

Some backstroke swimmers do butterfly kicks underwater after their turn, to help them go farther before they come back to the surface.

DIET

a good diet is important for everyone, not just swimmers. But competitive swimmers need to eat a lot more food in order to complete their rigorous training schedules – often several hours a day. While an average person should eat about 1,500–2,000 calories a day, swimmers sometimes eat up to four times this much.

NUTRITION

This diagram shows the percentage of foodstuff that should be eaten to maintain a balanced diet.

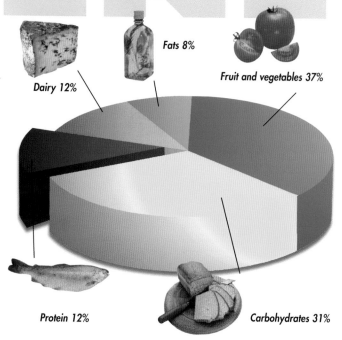

Fats 8%

Fruit and vegetables 37%

Dairy 12%

Protein 12%

Carbohydrates 31%

ENERGY BOOSTERS

If you are doing a lot of exercise, then you need to cut down on fatty foods and eat plenty of carbohydrates to provide the energy for the exercise you are doing.

Protein is required for the growth and repair of the body, but try to choose low-fat sources of it.

TOP TIP
Don't eat fatty foods in the 24 hours before a competition. They are slow to digest and will sit in your stomach for a long time.

FITNESS

p reparing yourself for a race means running through it in your mind beforehand. Block out all other distractions to make yourself 100 per cent focused. Flexibility is crucial for helping you to relax and taking your mind off the pressure. It will also help prevent injury. Above all, work on maintaining a high level of mental and physical fitness.

FLEXIBILITY

All top athletes need to keep their bodies flexible. It helps them avoid injury and improves their performance. Use the stretching exercises (*see pages 8–9*) to help increase your flexibility.

FIT FOR THE TOP

Most professional swimmers do other sports to give them all-round strength. Anything that keeps you fit and active can make a good break from swimming training.

MENTAL ATTITUDE

Winning a competition does not just rely on physical strength. It's a good idea to spend a little time before a race thinking through your starts, turns and tactics. Don't be distracted by other people and what they're doing; just concentrate on your own race.

TOP TIP

Don't do too much flexibility work – about 15 minutes every other day.

RACE TACTICS & EVENTS

One of the most important things when competing is that you swim your own race, instead of reacting to what someone else is doing. Here are a few hints on how to plan a race of 100 metres or more (shorter races are more or less 100 per cent speed all the way!)

COMPETITION RACING

STARTING
Start off fast, at about 95 per cent effort: your excitement will carry you through the first part of the race quicker than you think.

IN THE MIDDLE
The middle part of the race – lengths 2 and 3 of a 4-length race, for example – is the most important. This is where people often ease off, trying to save themselves for the finish.

THE TURN
Work hard on your turns to gain ground during the race. Turns should feel just as hard as the rest of the race!

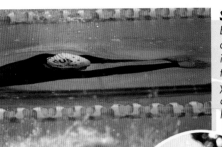

STAY AHEAD

Even if you are way ahead, put everything into the last section: there might be someone you haven't spotted very close behind. It might help you to imagine that there's a shark chasing you down the pool!

THE FINISH

Always time your strokes to swim right up to the wall instead of drifting in. Winning is often a matter of milliseconds so timing is crucial to beat the competition.

If you do your best time ever, it doesn't matter whether you come first or last. You're getting quicker, and one day you might be the quickest.

INDIVIDUAL EVENTS

These are the events that are featured in many international competitions. The rules are set by the Fédération Internationale de Natation Amateur (FINA).

m = metres

- *Front Crawl – 50 m, 100 m, 200 m, 400 m, 800 m, 1500 m.*

- *Backstroke – 50 m, 100 m, 200 m.*

- *Breaststroke – 50 m, 100 m, 200 m.*

- *Butterfly – 50 m, 100 m, 200 m.*

- *Individual Medley (all four strokes swum in the order of butterfly, backstroke, breaststroke, front crawl): 100 m (in a 25 m-long pool), 200 m, 400 m.*

TOP TIP

Don't keep looking around at the opposition: it will cost you time. Instead, focus on the wall at the end of the pool.

SWIMMING IN OTHER SPORTS

b eing a good swimmer isn't just useful if you want to enter races in the swimming pool. There are many other sports that require good swimming skills. Not only can it give you another interest, but it is one of the best ways to keep fit.

SYNCHRONIZED SWIMMING

Synchronized swimming is a combination of swimming and dance. Usually done as a team, the swimmers use a series of hand and leg movements to perform sequences. Timing is set by music and following other members of the group.

LONG-DISTANCE RACES

Some people enter long-distance races in the sea or even in rivers. Often these races are from one landmark to another – between two piers, or across a channel of water, for example.

BOARD DIVING

To be a successful diver you will need a coach. Each dive is split into three stages; take off, flight and entry. Marks are awarded for technique, style and ability.

DEEP-SEA DIVING

Divers need to be able to swim confidently. Otherwise they wouldn't be able to move around well on the bottom of the sea, or swim back to their boat if they ended up a long way away from it.

SURFING AND BODY BOARDING

Surfers and body boarders need to be strong swimmers for two reasons. Firstly they need to be able to get out through the breaking waves and white water to the area in which they catch waves. Secondly they need to be able to swim back to the beach through rough sea if they get separated from their board.

TRIATHLON & WATER POLO

*t*riathlon is becoming increasingly popular with people of all ages. It's one of the hardest sports in the world – one of the first competitions was called the 'Iron Man' contest! Another sport that is really good for strong swimmers is water polo, as it requires excellent swimming skills and strength to maintain play.

TRIATHLON EVENT

This triathlon took place at the Sydney Olympics in the year 2000. The events are continuous and can involve hundreds of people in one go!

LEG 1

The first part of the race is a swim. The distances vary from race to race, but a typical swim might be 800m (875 yds). This could be swum in a pool, a river, the sea or any other stretch of open water.

LEG 2

The racers then strip off their wetsuits and put on cycling shoes. They run to their bikes and set off: a typical ride might be for 25 km (15.5 miles).

LEG 3

The final stage is a run. The athletes leave their bikes and bike shoes, put on running shoes and set off. The run may be anywhere between 10-40 km (6-25 miles).

To play water polo you need to be a very good swimmer. The pace is fast and furious, where your feet cannot touch the ground! It is a little like football, except that it's played in a swimming pool. Each team has eleven players and the aim is to score as many goals as possible.

PLAYERS

Although the team is made up of eleven players, only seven are allowed to play at any one time. Every water polo team needs to have at least one fast sprinter!

PASSING

You need to be able to rise up out of the water to pass the ball well. If the ball goes out of the pool a free throw is awarded to the opposition.

SCORING

There are four five-minute matches with extra time if a goal is not scored. Goals are scored by throwing the ball into the back of the net.

WATER SAFETY

Never forget that water – any water that's deep enough to cover your face – is dangerous. The sea and rivers are especially deadly, and hundreds of people every year are drowned in them. But even swimming pools with lifeguards on duty see several deaths a year.

RIP CURRENTS

These dangerous currents claim many lives each year. They form where waves are breaking. If you are unlucky enough to be caught in one, stay calm and concentrate on getting out of the current. You can use the same technique to get out of other fast-flowing water.

Rip current flows out through deeper water

deep water

Undertow

Undertow

shallow water

STEP 1
Swim across the current: don't try to fight against it.

STEP 2
Once you are out of the current, swim back to shore.

WATER SAFETY – THE DO'S AND DONT'S...

DO

- Look out for warning signs

- Tell someone where you are going

- Obey notices and flags telling you where to swim

- Swim parallel to the shore, keeping it in sight at all times

- Get out of the water if it gets cold

DON'T

- Swim alone

- Swim near piers or in areas with strong currents

- Swim near boats or other water vessels

- Go out of your depth if you are not a proficient swimmer

- Dive into water less than 2 metres (6ft) deep; you may injure yourself

WARNING

If you're not certain that you can cope with the conditions, don't go into the sea. Surfers have an expression about this: 'If in doubt, don't go out.'

WARNING SIGNS

If you see this sign it means 'Do not swim'. A red flag means 'danger: do not enter the water'. Be sure to obey these warnings or you will put your own life in danger, as well as the life of the person who may have to rescue you.

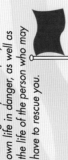

2.0m

Depth markers such as this one tell you in metres (or, on some older markers, in feet) how deep the water is. Never dive into water less than 2 metres deep, or any water in which there might be an obstruction.

LIFESAVING

earning the basic skills of lifesaving could, one day, save your life or the life of someone else. Most of water safety is common sense, but water is dangerous if not respected. Remember that play can turn into something much more serious in a matter of seconds.

RIVER RESCUE

It's very dangerous to wade into a fast-flowing river to rescue someone clinging to a rock or log. This is probably the least dangerous way to do it, if there are enough people.

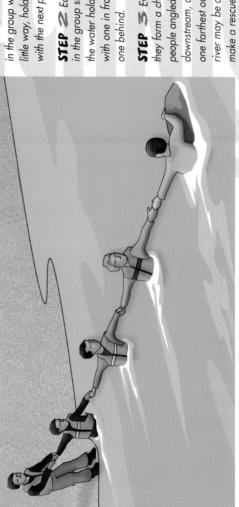

STEP 1 The first person in the group wades out a little way, holding hands with the next person.

STEP 2 Each person in the group steps into the water holding hands with one in front and one behind.

STEP 3 Eventually they form a chain of people angled slightly downstream, and the one farthest out in the river may be able to make a rescue.

WHAT TO DO IF...

...YOU ARE IN TROUBLE

- Stay calm
- Be decisive. Either:
  - float until someone arrives
  - tread water and wave one arm for assistance
  - if you swim back to safety, use the backstroke but with the breaststroke leg action to move faster. Being on your back will keep your head out of water, allowing you to breathe more easily

...SOMEONE ELSE IS IN TROUBLE

- Stay calm
- Shout for help or go and get help from someone else
- Do not go into the water without lifesaving training
- Use objects to rescue the person, without swimming towards them – you could both end up in trouble!

BASIC LIFESAVING

The key to rescuing someone is to ensure your own safety as well as that of the person in trouble. Details of basics lifesaving courses are available from your local swimming baths.

This swimmer is practising towing someone who needs rescuing. He is keeping his head out of the water and giving him a chance to breathe.

LIFEGUARDS

Lifeguarding can turn into a full-time job: some people are able to travel the world working as lifeguards. Even if you don't want to work as a lifeguard, it's a very useful skill to have. If you spot someone in the water in trouble, you will be able to help them.

HOW THE FAMOUS DO IT

b eing a competitive swimmer is very hard work. Few people ever get rich swimming – even the best swimmers struggle to make a living, and only Olympic gold medallists are able to earn large amounts of money from product endorsement and media interviews. As with most athletes, competitive swimmers take part in the sport because they love it.

TRAINING DIARY

6:00	Wake up. Drink cup of tea, fruit juice or water.
6:30 – 8:30	Training in the pool.
9:00 – 11:30	Eat breakfast: lots of carbohydrates, such as bread and jam, cereal and scrambled eggs.
12:00 – 1:00	Flexibility session, gym work or swim bench training.
1:30	Eat lunch - the biggest meal of the day: more carbohydrates, such as pasta, bread, and rice, but also protein (meat or fish) and vegetables.
5:30 – 7:00	Training in the pool.
8:00	Go home and rest.
10:00	Bedtime.

And the next day it starts all over again...

IAN THORPE–'THORPEDO'

Ian Thorpe won several gold medals at the 2000 Olympics. The most thrilling was the last stage of the men's 4 x 100m freestyle, in which Thorpe's Australian team beat the United States by a narrow margin. Thorpe overtook the American 100m specialist Gary Hall Jr in the last few strokes to snatch gold.

MONEY

Alexander Popov, the brilliant Russian sprinter, has been one of the world's best for over a decade. Popov is one of the few who make much money from swimming. Even people who make it to the Olympic finals sometimes struggle to fund their swimming.

REACHING THE OLYMPICS

Janet Evans is one of the United State's most successful women swimmers. To win Olympic gold medals, as Janet has, you have to work extremely hard. Even the best swimmers in the world don't win without training hard. There are lots of talented swimmers, and it's hard training that decides which of them wins the gold.

RACE-DAY DIARY

There are swimming clubs across the world that regularly hold national competitions, galas and international championships. This is a typical day for a swimmer in an inter-club gala.

6:00	*Wake up thinking you have to go training. Remember it's a race day and go back to sleep.*
9:00	*Get up: have some breakfast (not as much as usual) and drink plenty of juice or water. Avoid drinking too much tea or coffee.*
9:30 – 12:00	*Rest, perhaps doing a little flexibility work.*
12:30	*Eat a light lunch with lots of carbohydrates: avoid meat, cheese or fatty foods.*
3:00	*Travel to the gala.*
5:00	*Warm up.*
5:30	*The gala starts: swimmers wait for their race.*
8:30	*Gala finishes: go home and reflect on the high and low points of the race for next time.*

TOP TIP

Everyone on a team should cheer for one another. It makes each swimmer do better in their races, so it will help you do better in yours.

GLOSSARY

Armstroke – The action of your arms while swimming.

Dolphin Kick – The leg action used for the butterfly stroke.

Drag – Resistance in the water caused by clothing and hair.

Free start – When someone dives in before the gun has signalled the start of the race, it is called a false start. This will result in disqualification.

Gala – A set of swimming races taking place one after another.

Glide – The use of momentum to move through the water before commencing a stroke. Arms are held against the body with legs out to the back for a streamlined action.

Kick board – A float you hold on to while doing legs-only swimming.

Olympics – A sporting competition held every four years, where the best of the world's sportspeople, from many different sports, take part.

Overarm recovery – The part of your armstroke that takes place above water.

Pull buoy – A float that you tuck between your thighs to help you stay in the right position in the water when doing arms-only swimming.

Pull – The part of your armstroke that moves you forwards through the water.

Recovery – The point at which the arms or legs return to the starting position.

Starting block – A small, raised platform from which racing swimmers dive at the start of a race.

Triathlon – A race made up of swimming, cycling and running events.

Trickle breathing – Releasing the air in short bursts when underwater.

Tumble turn – A front crawl turn where your hands don't touch the wall. Instead, you duck down underwater and flip your feet over to hit the wall, then push off for your next length.

Two-arm recovery – The term given to the action of the arms above water during the butterfly stroke.

Underwater stroke – See pull.

LISTINGS

FINA
(Féderation Internationale De Natation Amateur)
The international governing body for swimming:
Ave. de l'Avant - Poste 4, 1005 Lausanne, Switzerland
Tel +41 (21) 310 47 10
Fax +41 (21) 312 66 10
www.fina.org.

ASA (Amateur Swimming Association)
The national governing body for swimming in Great Britain:
Harold Fern House, Derby Square, Loughborough, LE11 5AL, UK
Tel + 44 (0) 1509 618700
www.britishswimming.org.